P9-DTB-283

Smile

How Young Charlie Chaplin Taught the World to Laugh (and Cry)

Gary Golio

illustrated by Ed Young

CANDLEWICK PRESS

Once there was a boy named Charlie . . .
A little slip of a boy
With dark curly hair and deep-blue eyes
Who roamed the streets of London
Hungry for Life.
(And maybe a bit of bread!)

What he found:
Busy men in bowler hats
Laughing children with colored balloons
A flower seller with his jingly cart and horse
And penny steamboats racing up the Thames.
A feast of stories — which he gobbled right up!

🙼

Sometimes Charlie danced
For pennies
Outside a pub
Where a sad face and two happy feet
Earned him enough
For a toasted tea cake with jam.
Ahhh . . .

Charlie's parents were singers and actors
Though Dad left many years ago.
So Charlie lived with Mum
And older brother Sydney
In one small room with a bed.

Things weren't always this way. . . .

Charlie remembered:

Fancy rooms with a housemaid

Sweetcakes and candies

And a blue velvet suit with matching blue gloves.

Mum used to call him *the King*.

But that was before her singing voice quit —
One night at a smoky music hall —
And five-year-old Charlie
Waiting in the wings
Stepped in front of the footlights.

He sang —
And a shower of silver coins fell about him!
He scooped them up —
And the crowd roared with laughter!
He danced —
And the cheering got louder!

It was Charlie's first performance
And Mum's last.

Charlie didn't know whether to laugh or cry.

Now, when Mum wasn't sewing to make ends meet

She'd sit by the window

Spinning tales for Charlie

All about the people passing by.

The man with a big red nose was secretly a circus clown.

The lady with a feathered hat took her poodles for tea in the park.

Everyone had a story.

All the world's a stage.

At night, Mum would read Charlie a play before bedtime.

Acting each part in a different voice

She'd move and dance to bring characters alive.

Charlie would clap, beaming, from bed

And fall asleep dreaming

Of all he'd seen in his mind.

Yet try as Mum might, her money ran out —
And it was off to the poorhouse for her and the boys.
(Where at least there'd be some food!)

Heads were shaved, hands were slapped,
Mum went away with the nurses
Sydney with the older boys.
And little Charlie got very very lonely.

But when he learned to write his name

C-h-a-p-l-i-n

Those letters say me! he thought,
And his tears turned into a smile.

Chaplin

As Mum got stronger, things got better.
Out of the poorhouse, back on their own
She had Charlie practice a poem.
"Miss Priscilla's Cat"

His schoolteacher loved it, and Charlie recited it
To each and every class.
Howls of laughter! Peals of applause!
Little Charlie relished
The spotlight.

At nine, Charlie joined the Eight Lancashire Lads
A theater troupe for boys.
Those happy feet would earn some money once more!

In a white linen shirt and shiny red shoes
He clog-danced in theaters with clowns and comedians.
Everything he saw stuck in his mind—
Like

ZARMO *the*
Comedy Tramp Juggler
You'll laugh! You'll cry!

Then, dressed as a cat for a silent *Cinderella*
Charlie pretended to pee on the curtain.
The manager scowled. The audience howled.

HA HA HA
It was worth getting yelled at to make people smile!

When his days with the Lads were done
Charlie's face shone like the sun
Watching actors he knew meet and mingle
Outside the pub near his house.

Plus there was old Rummy Binks
Who held horses for a penny
While the carriage drivers took their meal.
Baggy clothes, turned-out feet, a crooked little cane.
Charlie mimed his wobbly walk for Mum
Who laughed but felt bad
Since she really thought Rummy quite sad.

And Charlie began to understand
How Funny and Sad went hand in hand.

Now, while Mum was sick
And Sydney in the Navy
Charlie took what jobs he could find.
As errand boy for a doctor.
Teaching dance to children.
Even making toy boats that he could sell for a penny.

Still, some days
He'd shed a tear or two
Just waiting for the sun to come
Brightly shining through.

But then . . .

The chance of a lifetime —
A plum part in a play!

Young Charlie Chaplin
IS BILLY THE PAGEBOY
IN
SHERLOCK HOLMES

Ah, little Charlie!

Critics loved him. Audiences adored him.
More than just acting
Now he was learning
To really make people *care*!

In several more plays
Charlie was funny, a *natural.*
He'd make people squeal just by
Stumbling, slipping, or taking a fall.

With his deep-blue eyes, he'd *hypnotize.*
With his body, he'd tell stories.

Just like Mum had done.

FRED KARNO'S COMPANIES

Then Charlie and Sydney began
Acting together, two brothers
In

Soon Charlie starred as a bumbling housepainter.
Buckets were falling! Ladders were flying!
Tumbling through the air, he'd land on his bum unhurt!
Though the audience felt sorry
They laughed till they cried
And loved every minute of mayhem.

Laughter and Tears were brothers, too.

One day, Mr. Karno told Charlie:
It's off to America, lad!
From the elegant East
To the wild wild West
Charlie toured the land 'cross the sea.

In New York City, he strode down Broadway
Under soaring skyscrapers and a thousand lights.
Still, it was somehow funny
That sad and lonely for home by day
Charlie made people laugh all night.

Starring in *A Night in an English Music Hall*
Charlie tipsied and tumbled all over the stage
Pretending to be older and drunk.
Audiences couldn't believe their eyes —
Was this fellow *real*?

But someone *did* believe his eyes —
Mack Sennett, famous filmmaker from California.
Soon, little Charlie from London
Was traveling by train to Hollywood
Where movies were new . . . and *silent*.
Shhh!

But when Mack met Charlie
(Without any makeup)
He wasn't so sure.
Chaplin's so young! Can this guy deliver?

Though Charlie proved funny
In movie #1
Mack wanted *funnier*
For movie #2.
He said:
Put on some makeup.
Anything will do.

But Charlie felt sure
He needed something *more* —
A funny face alone wouldn't do.

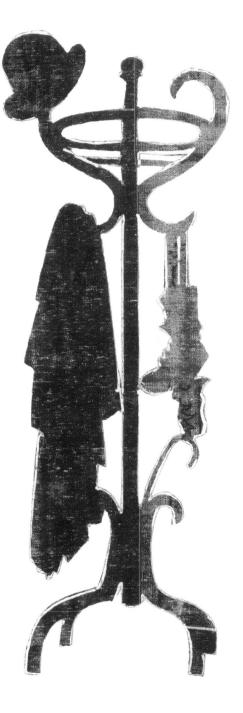

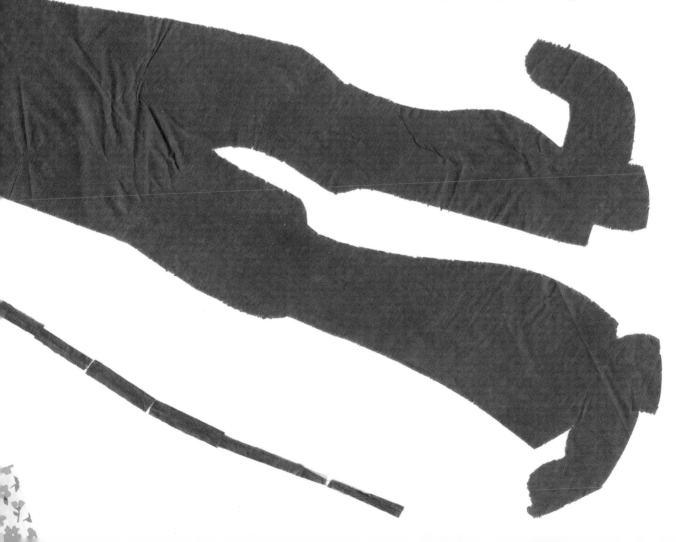

Alone in the prop room
He rummaged
Through dusty clothes
And memories.

What Charlie found:
Some baggy old pants
A tiny topcoat
Beat-up shoes (too big)
And a black bowler hat.

The makings of a tramp.

Then he glued on a mustache
Grabbed a crooked old cane
And was suddenly something *more*.

Someone who'd make the world
Laugh and cry . . .

A funny little fellow named

Charlie

✿

To the
Master of Silence
Laughter
&
Tears

G. G.

To the great wizard
Who lets us see
Light in all darkness
Beauty in the mundane
Music in quietude
Joy in every deprivation
Or vice versa

E. Y.

Afterword

❦

"I had no idea of the character. But the moment I was dressed, the clothes and the make-up made me feel the person he was. I began to know him, and by the time I walked onto the stage he was fully born."[1]

— Charlie Chaplin on the Tramp

Without Charlie Chaplin, there probably wouldn't be movies the way we know them today. He found a way to make us laugh and cry in the same film, to make us care about the characters and their adventures. Actor, writer, director, composer, songwriter, editor, producer, and distributor—he was the first to do it all, and he did it masterfully.

By 1915—within a year of Charlie acting in his first movie—his character the Little Tramp was the most famous "person" in the world. The Tramp was small, strange-looking, poor, hungry, and lonely: somebody people would laugh at or just ignore. He didn't quite fit in, and things didn't always go his way. Usually he lost what he'd found—money, a job, food, or a girl—and ended up with nothing. It was tough being the Little Fellow . . . but somebody had to do it!

In Charlie's Little Tramp character, what seemed like weakness often turned out to be strength. What was a problem became a solution. A lot of work—by Charlie Chaplin the actor—made what the Tramp did on film look easy. It was child's play, after all, but done by a grown-up. And he didn't have to speak a word!

1. Chaplin, *My Autobiography*, p. 144.

As Charlie Chaplin himself said: "You know this fellow is many-sided, a tramp, a gentleman, a poet, a dreamer, a lonely fellow, always hopeful of romance and adventure. He would have you believe he is a scientist, a musician, a duke, a polo player. However, he is not above picking up cigarette butts or robbing a baby of its candy. And, of course, if the occasion warrants it, he will kick a lady in the rear — but only in extreme anger!"[2]

You see, Charlie wasn't afraid to act like a child. To show us how someone small could be clever and strong. To let us laugh at him so we could laugh at ourselves. To make us cry so we could feel bigger, more alive, and more human. In other words, Charlie Chaplin had the courage to be funny. And that's why we love him. Because more than anything else, he is us.

"No matter how desperate the predicament is, I am always very much in earnest about clutching my cane, straightening my derby hat and fixing my tie, even though I have just landed on my head."[3]
— Charlie Chaplin

2. Chaplin, *My Autobiography*, p. 144.
3. Charles Chaplin, "What People Laugh At," *American Magazine*, November 1918.

Facts About Charlie Chaplin

He was born in England in 1889, lived and worked in America for forty years, and then moved to Switzerland, where he died in 1977 at the age of eighty-eight.

Both his parents were entertainers: his mother a singer, his father a singer and actor. His half-brother Sydney was not only an actor but also Charlie's manager later on.

As children, Charlie and Sydney were placed in workhouses for the poor because their mother was very ill and couldn't take care of them.

Charlie started acting when he was about nine. One of his earliest roles was in the stage play *Sherlock Holmes*, as Billy the pageboy.

On a tour of America in 1912 with the Karno Company, Charlie was seen and "discovered" by early filmmaker Mack Sennett, creator of the Keystone Cops comedies.

Acting in his first movie at age twenty-four, in 1914 (he made thirty-five movies that first year!), Charlie was a sudden success. His Little Tramp character made his feature-film debut in 1915 and became a worldwide sensation. "Chaplinitis" took over America—with songs, dances, comic books, and Tramp look-alike contests. It's said that Charlie even entered one himself — and lost!

Charlie began directing feature-length movies in 1915. In 1918, he was given a million dollars to make eight films. Two of them were among his greatest: *A Dog's Life* (1918) and *The Kid* (1921).

Charlie made and/or acted in more than eighty movies, working until he was nearly eighty years old. He often wrote, starred in, directed, edited, produced, and composed the music for his films.

One of the most beautiful melodies he composed was for the song "Smile." Lyrics were added later, and the song has been recorded by countless performers, including Michael Jackson.

Resources

To watch Charlie Chaplin's movies, borrow them from your local library or search the Internet, including YouTube. The following are especially well suited to children:

The Kid (1921) • *The Circus* (1928) • *The Fireman* (1916)
A Dog's Life (1918) • *The Gold Rush* (1925)

PHOTO FROM THE NEW YORK PUBLIC LIBRARY

Selected Books and Movies

Ackroyd, Peter. *Charlie Chaplin: A Brief Life*. New York: Nan A. Talese/Doubleday, 2014.

Chaplin, Charles. *The Chaplin Revue*. Burbank, CA: MK2/Warner Home Video, 2004. DVD boxed set.

———. *My Autobiography*. New York: Simon and Schuster, 1964.

Fleischman, Sid. *Sir Charlie: Chaplin, the Funniest Man in the World*. New York: Greenwillow, 2010.

Robinson, David. *Chaplin: His Life and Art*. New York: Da Capo, 1994.

Vance, Jeffrey. *Chaplin: Genius of the Cinema*. New York: Abrams, 2003.

You may also want to visit the official Charlie Chaplin website: www.charliechaplin.com

First edition 2019

Library of Congress Catalog Card Number 2018961167
ISBN 978-0-7636-9761-7

18 19 20 21 22 23 CCP 10 9 8 7 6 5 4 3 2 1

Printed in Shenzhen, Guangdong, China

This book was typeset in Pabst Oldstyle.
The illustrations were done in collage and ink.

Candlewick Press
99 Dover Street
Somerville, Massachusetts 02144

visit us at www.candlewick.com